MONETALIA:
The Guide to Achieve Financial Success

Table of Contents

Introduction 1

Chapter One: The Power That the Thoughts
Have on Financial Success 4

Chapter Two: The Power Desire Has
on Financial Success 10

Chapter Three: The Principle of Persistence 16

Chapter Four: A Practical Step by Step Guide
to Manifest Money Successfully 20

Chapter Five: The Best Ways to Improve
Your Finance 25

Chapter Six: The Four Deadly Sins of
Your Personal Finance 29

BONUS Chapter: Things That Millionaires
Won't Tell You but Will Agree Definitely On. 34

Conclusion 39

Book Disclaimer 41

Introduction

This is a self-improvement, psychological book with the goal to improve your current financial situation. The book's title *'Monetalia'* comes from the Latin term for money *'moneta'*.

Monetalia is divided into two parts – a psychological and a practical part. The author's goal behind this is to give the reader two perspectives. The first part, the psychological, discusses the details about the power of the mind on your current financial situation. However, the author believes that psychological advice without practical advice is completely useless. That's why the second part talks about useful practices you can incorporate into your everyday life.

The first part is divided into 3 important chapters. These chapters want you to understand the power that your mind has in your everyday life. This is pure psychological advice. The chapters are the following:

- The Power That the Thoughts Have on Financial Success

Introduction

- The Power Desire Has on Financial Success
- The Principle of Persistence

The second, practical part talks about ways that you can actually improve your finance. More precisely, how to manifest money, how to improve income and minimize spending. These chapters are:

- A Practical Step by Step Guide to Manifest Money Successfully
- The Best Ways to Improve Your Finance
- The Four Deadly Sins of Your Personal Finance

The book ends with a special 'bonus chapter' called:

- Things That Millionaires Won't Tell You but Will Agree Definitely On.
- The Way Rich People Think

You may be thinking, how could this be possible if my view of myself is that of a failure? Or you may even think, why on earth does fear seem to have such a hold or grasp on me? Where did all of this type of thinking come from? Why can't I seem to move on with my life and be totally free and whole as a person?

Well, I know that fear certainly didn't come from the heart of God because God is love and loves us all with an everlasting love that is unconditional. His thoughts of you is what truly matters, not what you think of yourself or of what others may think of you. He created you and He makes no mistakes. He builds a masterpiece of people's lives.

There is such a striving in this old world for attention and significance when really we are to live for our audience of one. He has never called us to live in bondage in becoming people pleasers. God, the Father is the only one we need to please. He has called us to move into a close and intimate relationship with Him and longs for us to spend those precious times with Him in His presence.

CHAPTER ONE

The Power That the Thoughts Have on Financial Success

It is widely known that thoughts can be very powerful and preemptive. The thoughts that you have in your own mind can help you to shape your life without having the conscious realization of it happening. Most people do not understand the great power that thoughts have.

- *"Change your thoughts, and you change your world"*

These are the words of a former American minister and author Norman Vincent Peale. He was a best-selling author for the self-improvement book *"The Power of Positive Thinking"* and obviously he knows a thing or two about achieving financial success.

The truth is, we all are products of our thoughts. **Think, and you shall become.** Your way of thinking is a large part of the manifestation of your destiny. Not everyone has understood this however, since most people do not believe in the amazing power their thoughts have. Most people do not understand that the very things they are thinking about are slowly coming to them.

Talking from a biological side of view, thoughts are energy. They move through the synapses of our brains, since they move from one neuron to another in lightning-fast speed. It's almost an instantaneous process. Just imagine, you think about moving your hand, and as you think, it happens. Unlike computers, where you have to wait for the processor to send the directives, your mind has no limitations. It is the most powerful computer in the world.

Think about it, the energy that moves across your synapses and neurons has the power to change your life, either for better or for worse. Just one single thought, one spark of neuron activity is enough to make you do something. This one choice that you made will change the path you move, either directing you towards your hopes and dreams, or sending you on your path to failure. These same thoughts also manifest in our minds, changing our behavior and emotions until it matches reality.

You cannot hide the fact that your thoughts hold incredible power. They can be used either for good or bad. But what are your thoughts exactly? How do they work? How can we use them for the better? Is our current situation like this due to our thoughts?

The human mind is a subject in anatomy that we still don't know too much about. With our current level of scientific development, we really don't know how does consciousness work and just how complex our mind truly is. These are some facts that we can't quite wrap our heads around yet.

Our lives are the product of our thoughts, not the other way around. To prove this, we can state that there have been multiple studies where two identical twins have grown to become completely different people. From a biological perspective, these two people are exact copies, so they should have relatively similar lives, right? Guess what makes them take different live paths. **That's right – their thoughts.**

Okay, I believe now that your quite bored, reading about neurons, thoughts and identical twins. We know that your goal is to **achieve financial success.** So, we will strive to make this book as practical as possible, meaning that you can apply a lot of rules to your everyday life. So, to begin, we will write three daily thoughts that you should think about. These thoughts will improve your thinking and overtime, boost your successes:

1. *"My financial situation will improve"*

This is a big one. If you are in a big debt, or you lost your house to an earthquake, it can be quite difficult for you to think positively. But, it is important to remember that with time and effort you **CAN** change your situation for the better. They key word here is **CAN.** Things (usually) don't improve by themselves. A lot of time, effort and energy **WILL** be wasted just to improve your financial situation, but, in the long run, **it will be worth it.**

2. "I must stay persistent and patient"

We cannot emphasize enough that **good things take time.** Sometimes, this can be a lot of time. Life can be extremely hard at moments, even unbearable, making you want to give up. The true path is to stay persistent no matter what. Remember, someone once said:

- **"A winner is just the loser who never gave up."**

You can be this "loser who never up". Even though at moments of hardship, sentences like *"Stay Strong"* and *"Stay Persistent"* can feel useless, you must understand that you have to keep pushing. It's all in your mind. It always has been and it always will be. **More on persistence later.**

3. "I have no limitations"

Look, if someone is setting limitations on you, it is most likely yourself. Life will present you with quite a lot of moments; some of them unbearably hard, and some of them will be chances that you can't let go. We will give you a very useful example. This is a true story backed up by science. Please read:

> *"When an elephant is young, its trainer puts a chain around its leg, restraining it from moving too far away. The young elephant will initially try to escape, wanting to roam the wild and remove any limitation. After a while, this young animal will realize that it is not capable of escaping, enabling the trainer to control him for the rest of his life. As the elephant grows up to an adult size, weighing anywhere from 3,000 to 6,000 kilograms, it still believes that the chain is holding him, so it won't even try to break free, even though it is capable of escaping with just a little effort. These animals could break free at any time, but they are limited because of their beliefs."*

Just like these elephants, many of us go through life believing that we cannot do something, simply because we have failed once at it. How many people are being held by their old beliefs, thinking that they are not capable of doing something?

Please remember – **Whatever you can believe, you can achieve.**

We recommend that the three aforementioned sentences should become a part of your everyday life. Please write them on a paper, and just put them on any place in your home that you visit frequently (example your mirror). Over time, this will manifest, taking over a part of your mind, and eventually forcing you to grow at an unprecedented rate.

CHAPTER TWO

The Power Desire Has on Financial Success

Desire is what fuels success. If you do not have the desire to succeed in any area in your life, whether it's sport, financial success, marriage or anything else, you will not achieve it. A goal without a desire is like a car driving without gas. In simple terms, you won't go anywhere.

Do you want to know a practical example of how desire influences the world? Have you wondered why many professional athletes lose to a weaker and inferior opponent? Just recently last year, the 100m sprint champion Usain Bolt lost his reign over the Olympic sprinting. He lost to someone who was almost 5 years older than him, less physically capable and Bolt was heavily favored by the public. Do you know the reason behind his loss? **That's right, his desire.** Since Bolt was the reigning champion for multiple years in a row, he was not as **HUNGRY** for success in comparison to the other players. You will understand this shortly.

Most people who want to achieve financial success either don't have the large enough desire to succeed, or they have lost their desire. If you want to achieve your goals you must have a large desire to do it. One of the most important questions you can ask yourself is – *What is my desire?*

Let's face it, we, as humans, want many different things in life. But **wanting** and **desiring** are two completely different things. Realizing and understanding the core behind your desire is absolutely critical to your success. We will state a couple of examples of many people who had very clear desires and goals:

- Muhammad Ali had a burning desire to be the heavyweight champion of the world
- Bill Gates had a deep desire for a computer to exist in every single household in the world
- Warren Buffet really desired to make a lot of money by investing
- Nelson Mandela wanted to free all of the blacks in South Africa

All of these people had a very deep desire that fueled their ability to succeed. Mike Tyson is an excellent example of a man who had lost his desire. He said once in a public interview:

> *"I lost my desire. I am not hungry anymore. I'm wealthy, my kids have money and I have nothing to fight for."*

Tyson had a very deep desire to fight. He also wanted to be wealthy and for his family to be financially secure. His real goal was to achieve **financial success.** Since he had the money, it wasn't necessary for him to fight anymore. If he wanted to make money again, we would have come back, made a public appearance, stage a fight between him and a popular boxer, and make a couple million dollars just like that. I bet you had enough of this "desire" crap. Since the goal behind making this book was very practical, we now think that we should tell you, the reader, how to direct your desires properly. Look, first, it is necessary to comprehend that when you have a desire, you have the power to fuel your body with new abilities, and receive assistance from your subconscious mind to achieve your goals. As long as you have the desire, you will have the power to do the thing that you have imagined.

You have probably heard a story from some survivor who somehow overcame even the worst odds to survive. Some people have been trapped for days without water, and months without food, but somehow, in the end, they survived. You know what kept them alive? **The desire to**

live. Many doctors and scientists will agree on this, that people who lose their desire to live, will die much more quickly than people who still have a desire to live life.

Some of you might say *"I really don't know what I desire"* or *"How do I manifest a desire"* because maybe, you still don't have a deep one inside of you. Look, it is really simple. First, you must look at what areas in your life require improvement. This can be your romantic situation, your bank account, your weight, or anything else. What's important is that you see what needs improvement. Let's say that you believe that your financial situation requires improvement.

Learning about your desire is the first step of achieving your final goal. Recently, we asked someone about his desires, and he said: *"I really want to become rich"*. Okay, that seems understandable. But it is absolutely necessary for him to understand **why** he wants to become rich. Those people who want to become rich want to achieve: *more freedom, a luxurious lifestyle, less stress or even a nice car.* These are their end goals, these are the things they **really desire.**

The next step to achieving the goal of financial success is to improve your lifestyle and attitude. This will allow you to fulfill your desire. If you want to be rich, but all you do is lay in the bed, we apologize in advance but **you will not be rich.** You **MUST** get your body to work, whether it's manual labor, entrepreneurship, or anything else. If you adopt anything from this book, please adopt the following suggestions that we will give you:

- **Always** keep a pen and a notepad in your pocket. Use this to write down your thoughts, words and actions. When you catch yourself thinking about a goal, whether is business, or marriage, just write it down. This will help you find your desire and manifest it in your mind.
- Once your desire become a little clearer, you must instruct your subconscious mind to create the circumstances to achieve your goals. Remember this *–lifewill give you a chance, it is your job to take it and do your best.*
- If you have the clear desires and proper instructions from your subconscious mind, it is unavoidable to say that you are **unstoppable.**

You can improve your life drastically. If you take anything from this book, please let take the aforementioned suggestions. You **CAN** improve your life. Life will give you chances to achieve anything, whether it is success, happiness, romance or health. Once you take control of your thoughts (chapter 1) and direct your desires (chapter 2) you can start changing your life by the day. Start doing this today, don't waste any moment that leads you in the wrong direction.

Remember, **this is the only life you have.** This is it. Use the most out of your potential to make the maximum out of it. You give only one life and one chance.

CHAPTER THREE

The Principle of Persistence

If you look anywhere in the world, in almost every industry, culture or country, you will see a consistent trend that almost all successful individuals have – **persistence.** That's right. Almost everyone who is successful has persisted way beyond what was expected from them.

Of course, persistence is a learned trait. These people weren't born to be persistent naturally. Instead, they learned it throughout their lives. Persistence is a choice. It is the matter of believing in yourself and finding ways to maneuver through a situation even when all previous attempts failed. Perseverance is the true mark of the champions. Those who do not quit are the ones who achieve great things.

Perseverance is the ability to attempt to do something even when you are constantly being criticized, or when you're constantly losing. However, this is the trait that separates the winners from the losers. When an individual sets his focus on something particular, and he does everything to achieve that goal, he will usually get what he wants.

Even though it might not look simple, this is an extremely easy principle to follow. If you know what you want, you will get it *only if* you pursue it relentlessly. Is it that simple, you might ask? The answer is an absolute **yes.** I dare you to read stories of the ones who have achieved a great measure of success, and see if they applied this principle. You will see that if you refuse to quit, sooner or later, you will find the thing that you pursue.

Now, we will look at examples of people that have successfully beat defeat and have pursued their goals. They have been very persistent even through the most difficult times:

- **Abraham Lincoln**

He failed in business at age 21. He was defeated in a legislative race at 22. He failed in business one more time at age 24. He was faced with the death of his lover at age 26. He had a nervous breakdown at age 27. Lost a race in congress at age 34, and yet again at 36. Lost a senatorial race at 45. Failed to become vice president at 47. Lost a senatorial race at 49 yet again. *He was finally elected as the president of the United States at age 52.* Imagine what the world would look like if he hadn't persisted through all of his previous failures.

- **Thomas Edison**

He tried 9,999 times to perfect the light bulb, and each time he failed. Someone close to him asked him *"Are you going to have 10,000 failures?"* He simply responded – *"I did not fail, I just discovered another way not to invent the electric light bulb"*. You see, Edison chose to perceive his previous experiences **not as failures.**

- **Colonel Sanders**

Colonel Sanders is The Founder of KFC (Kentucky Fried Chicken). He was a military retiree and had nothing to do, except cook chicken from his mother's recipe. So what did he do? He took his old wagon, and began driving to restaurant after restaurant. His intention was to sell his chicken recipe. He was rejected a whopping **1,007 times**before he received his first yes. This is how KFC began.

- **Steve Jobs**

He was the CEO of Apple, one of the wealthiest corporations in the world. Members of his own board of directors kicked him out of his own company. He could have allowed this to stop him, but instead, he came back to Apple, and later became the chairman. Later, he created the iPod, the iPhone and a brand new line of Mac computers. Today, the technological world is unthinkable without an iPhone.

As you can see, time and time again, these individuals were stopped by difficulties along their journey. Just because they failed doesn't mean that their failures defined them or that their dreams and projects would never exist. Instead, just because they were persistent, they found **one more way it does not work** – as Edison believed. However, this meant that they were one step closer to achieving their results.

CHAPTER FOUR

A Practical Step by Step Guide to Manifest Money Successfully

Since you have read the previous three chapters, we now believe that you know that you know that you can attract money with the power of your thoughts and desires. However, there might be multiple things in your life that hold you back from successfully manifesting money into your life. This will be a very practical chapter that includes a step by step guide that will teach you about the most effective techniques for successful manifestation.

First, let's talk about something that might prevent you from successfully manifesting money. The number one reason most people fail to successfully manifest money is due to the way they **perceive** cash. Many people see their jobs as a source of stress and concern, building up a lot of **anxiety** in their lives. However, it is absolutely necessary to get rid of negative thoughts and feelings to be fully capable of the job you want. Manifesting money is a process that is supposed to be positive, optimistic and cheerful. Enough with philosophies, let's get to the guide:

1. Understand the reason why you need money

This is extremely important. Many people want a "pile of money" in their pocket. However, this is a desire that holds no real meaning. What is the reason behind your will to earn money? Is it to get a luxurious car? Is it to buy a new house? Maybe your wish is to travel?

Make sure to be 100% confident in your wish to earn money. Thinking that "having a lot of money" will solve your problems is just a very childish perception of the world. Make sure to write the reasons why you need money on a paper, and try to write as many things as you can.

2. Decide the precise amount of money you want to have

Most people need "many millions of dollars". That is a very vague statement that holds no true meaning. The majority of these people don't even know what it takes to have millions of dollars. It is important to the specific sum of money you require (example, $50,000). Once you achieve this, you can move up the ladder.

- *Note: Set short-term goals.*

3. Stop limiting yourself

We have talked about this previously. But, it cannot be overstated how much of a burden limitation can put on you. These are the thoughts that you should try to eliminate from your psyche:

- *My family is not rich, therefore I will not be rich*
- *The chances for me to become rich are really low*
- *Money is the root of evil*

Look, every time you put a limitation to yourself, please think of the elephant example that you read about in chapter 1.

4. Possess the mindset of a rich person

You will **never** manifest money in your mind if you think like a poor person. You will be required to act as if you are wealthy. This does not mean spending money on useless things. It means allowing yourself to think on luxurious and expensive things once in a while.

5. Motivate yourself

This is also a key step on your way to financial freedom. It literally takes you 15 minutes to find 40-50 quotes that will motivate you. Write these down, and keep them in your household. They will awake very beautiful feelings in you. Some key locations to place these papers/images:

- Your office.
- Your bedroom.
- Your bathroom.
- Your kitchen.

Make sure that they are easily visible on places that you frequently visit. You will be glad.

6. VISUALIZE

Everyone who has ever achieved his goals has visualized them. This is a fact. Visualization is one of the keys to successful manifestation. Make sure to make your visualizations are as real as possible.

Try to imagine yourself with the money in your pocket, driving your favorite car, in the city you love the most. This is a proven technique that has been used by top-level athletes who have successfully become what they have envisioned.

7. Be prepared for what it takes to earn money

Earning a lot of money will not be easy. This is a fact. Becoming rich is something that will require *late nights, early mornings, hard work, dedication and time.* However, every time you are ready to give up on your dreams, please remember what your life would be like *if you were bankrupt.*

If you haven't watched the movie *"The Wolf of Wall Street"* we highly recommend that you do. In a very famous scene, Leonardo DiCaprio says:

> *"There is no nobility in poverty. I've been a poor man, and I've been a rich man. And I choose rich every single time."*

8. Be grateful for the money you already have

Even though it might not be very much, make sure to express gratitude for the money you already have. Your situation can always be worse. Keep a journal to yourself, and write down:

- *"I am grateful for the money I currently have"*.

- *"This amount of money makes me sleep peacefully"*.

Everyone has a different sense of gratitude. Make sure yours is honest and truthful, because if it's not, the universe will take even the smallest amount of money you have, for the reason of not expressing gratitude.

You have done an excellent job finishing the third chapter reader! Please make sure to practice these techniques every single day. Even though progress might be slow, you will be on a great path to transform your life.

CHAPTER FIVE

The Best Ways to Improve Your Finance

Concerns about your finance are one regular source of stress that you probably receive every day. It is important to remember that worrying usually does not solving anything by itself, but asking yourself the question on how to **maximize earnings** and **minimize spending** will lead you one step closer to overcoming your financial problems. There is a term someone once mentioned called *"financial literacy"*. This means being *literate* in the way that you are spending your finances. Put it in simple terms, **you need to know what you're doing.**

You can classify spending as a habit. Earning is also a habit. Most people have both **bad** and **good** habits. Your financial situation is a direct result of the **financial habits** you own. Trying to minimize the bad ones, and maximize the good ones will definitely assist you on the way of financial success. Let's get to them:

1. Track your incomes and expenses

We are starting off here with a big one. This means that you understand your relationship with money. The "pen and paper" example has been written out multiple times before, but we would also recommend that you use it here. Write out on a paper *how much you earn* and write down every single expense that you have, *from toilet paper to lottery tickets.*

2. Have a well-planned budget that you stick to

Once you have set a conclusion on the amount of money you earn and spend, the next key is managing your finances properly. Make sure to pay attention to every single detail and plan all of your expenses, both the bigger and the smaller ones.

3. Avoid going on shopping sprees at all costs

This means that you never buy anything on impulse. Shopping sprees can be a large negative factor to your budget, making you unaware of the last $1,000 you've spent.

4. Keep the money in your wallet to a minimum

This is a psychological one. Many scientific studies have concluded that humans *definitely* spend more when they have more money in their pockets.

5. Take advantage of small financial services

These can be some small, yet useful habits that you can adopt. This means that you become a very effective shopper, meaning that you **maximize coupons** and **savings.** Also, try to cut costs by taking on DIY (do-it-yourself) projects and prioritizing the most important expenses, for example food and travel.

6. Spend less on clothes

For all of the "fashion models", this might be a big problem. Clothing can suck your money out like a vacuum cleaner, seriously. However, there is a way to limit spending on clothes without sacrificing your style. Try to buy slightly off-season clothes, maybe even resort to using second-hand clothes. What many millionaire CEOs do is a very minimalistic approach. This means getting 5 simple t-shirts, 2 pairs of jeans and 2 jackets that are minimalistic and simple to wear.

7. Be prepared for financial disasters

Okay, maybe "disaster" is a hard word to use, but major financial accidents can happen way more frequently than you might think. Your business **will** probably fail the first time, since more than 80% of business *do in fact **fail**.* This means being prepared and *always* having a plan B.

8. Building up your savings

Elizabeth Warren, which is an American politician and academic senior senator from the United States, has made a very famous money plan. This money plan is called the *"50/30/20 rule".* This is how the plan works:

- 50% goes for **needs** – this means groceries, housing, utilities, insurance and car maintenance
- 30% goes for **wants** – this means shopping, dining, hobbies and overall relaxation
- 20% goes for **savings.**

9. Find a way to use social media to improve your finances

Social media tools can be one surprising way to manage your finances. Just tweeting to a retailer about a customer service problem can be one of the fastest ways to receive a response, sometimes even a full refund.

CHAPTER SIX

The Four Deadly Sins of Your Personal Finance

In this chapter, you will learn about the four deadly sins of personal finance and the way that they will make you go bankrupt. As we've already mentioned before, it is extremely important that you stick to your budget and have a clear goal. However, many of you might be surprised from the impact these four deadly sins have. Be wary, because these sins could easily destroy your budget and completely impair your ability to save money. These things are the biggest obstacles that are preventing you from sticking to your budget. They will definitely lead to financial doom. Many people lost their budgets precisely to these four deadly sins. Beware of the misery that they can bring to your budget. These are:

1. Cigarettes

The cost of smoking is not only a daily financial cost, but it also leads to higher costs for health and life insurance, healthcare costs due to smoking-related illnesses, and even have a negative impact on your loved ones.

If you are an average smoker in Washington, a pack of cigarettes costs you around $7. Multiply that by a pack a day – you get just over $200 monthly! That could be money spent on a flight ticket or a gym membership. Ultimately, these $200 monthly could be better in the bank rather than in your lungs.

Just calculate, if you smoke $7 a day, $200 monthly, $1400 annually, that's around **$12.000** over a five year period! That money could definitely be used to start your own business. Cigarettes are completely useless people…

Also, secondhand smoke has a negative effect on your loved ones, co-workers and friends. Really, no good stuff ever came from these things. They are just incredibly expensive and bad for your health.

2. Gambling

Gambling can have a very destructive effect on personal finances. Attempting to manage your losses can be almost impossible. Gamblers have a problem with spending their entire wages, gambling savings, acquiring debts etc. Take this example:

"Paul from Chicago was a successful 42-year old attorney. He began gambling as a way to deal with his boredom and loneliness. His wealthy situation allowed him to gamble for many years straight, seemingly with no consequences. Over time, he lost a lot of money, the credit ran up and he got depressed. Because of this, his overall financial, emotional and physical health had been destroyed, as well as his work performance. He had lost everything that he fought for over 20 years. His employer decided to fire him."

When gambling becomes uncontrollable, the gambler will spend even more money, attempting to **win back their losses.** This is definitely the most fatal tactic.

Just imagine, gambling $25 weekly for 5 years would make you lose around **$6.000.** Even if you win from gambling, this will be money that you will never love and spend cautiously, since you never earned it with a lot of work.

3. Alcohol

In addition to damaged health, strained relationships and lost productivity, alcohol has a large negative effect on your **finances** as well. You may not realize this soon enough, until your spending problem becomes really severe. If you are a frequent drinker, it's important to look at the obvious cost of drinking.

An occasional beer will definitely not leave you bankrupt, however, drinking habitually will definitely lead to a much larger alcohol bill. In addition to the pure cost of alcohol, drinking too much impacts your spending in other ways as well:

- You might spend extra cash unwisely, like ordering more snacks
- Your productivity of work will definitely suffer. Drinkers have a habit to show up sick frequently, as well as be under-slept.
- Your medical expenses will also rise. Alcohol effects your immune system negatively, making you more prone to get sick.

Drinking just $10 weekly will lead you to a loss of around **$2.500** in a span of five years. This will be money only spent on alcohol, not considering the extra money you will spend unwisely.

4. Dining out

Seriously, dining out can be horrendously expensive for anyone. In fact, compared to home cooked meals, dining out is **five times** more expensive. If you are trying to build up your budget you should not eat at a restaurant more than once or twice a month.

Dining out for $20 weekly over a five year period leads you to a loss of around **$5.000.**

Now, do a sum of all of the amounts of money that these four deadly sins qill make you lose. **$12.000 + $6.000 + $2.500 + $5.000 = over $25.000.** I don't know about you, but I'd rather spend $25.000 starting 5 different business with $5.000 each. Just remember that these $25.000 are the **minimum** you will spend over five years!

BONUS CHAPTER

Things That Millionaires Won't Tell You but Will Agree Definitely On.

By definition, millionaires are the people who have at least 1 million in dollars in their bank accounts. The latest reports have found out that in the world, there are just around 40 million people who are millionaires. That's definitely a lot of people. I bet that you won't recognize a millionaire just by looking at him on the streets. In fact, most millionaires look like anything but millionaires.

Nevertheless, here are some things that millionaires will definitely agree on but won't tell you:

1. They spend less than they earn

Obviously! This is their way of thinking. In the long run, they save up way more than the average person. That's the way they've successfully accumulated their wealth in the first place.

2. They are patient

They know that accumulating a million dollars is not a quick process. They are very well aware that money will gradually increase if you save and invest properly over multiple years and decades.

3. They are cheap

I bet that most millionaires don't drink coffee at coffee shops. These guys are incredibly cheap. Jeff Bezos who was reported to be the richest man in the world in 2018 drove his 1987 Chevy Blazer until he had more than $12 billion.

4. They pay their credit cards every month

This is where it's very important to understand that you should not buy things that you cannot afford completely. Most millionaires will agree that they use cash money the vast majority of the time since they find it more practical

5. They realized the concept of financial freedom

Financial freedom is a big concept that many strive to achieve. These guys have realized that the most crucial step to financial freedom is being **debt free.** That's it folks.

6. They know that having a second job will do you wonders

Not only does a second job (which will be part-time) increase your monthly earnings, but it also keeps you busy for a big chunk of the week. Having less time means that you will have less time to spend what you already have.

7. They understand that money requires proper management

Money cannot manage itself. It is necessary to understand that every single income requires some form of stable money management. Whether you do it yourself, or you employ someone else to do it for you, money should definitely be managed with skill.

8. They understand the importance of planning

Very few in the world have become millionaires accidentally. Most millionaires reached the million dollar milestone with a very detailed, and not only because of dumb luck. **Failing to plan is planning to fail.**

9. They think big

Every millionaire will agree that financial success demands that you have a very big vision. A vision that is a lot greater than what you are currently capable of.

10. They are ready for unplanned disasters

Bad stuff happen to everybody. A divorce, death of a loved one, disability that leads to a loss of work. These are stuff that can happen to almost anyone, and you should be prepared in such case.

11. They are not impressed by luxury

Your over-priced luxury car will not impress him. He knows that these things are just for show, and he has done the same as well.

12. They don't quit easily

Persistence is key friends. If you are willing to go up the market, you must be ready to fight the rules and not give up easily. These guys don't quit negotiating until they get the deal that they want.

13. They are ready for risk

Millionaires will definitely agree that the path for success is not a very safe path. Ups and downs have happened multiple times in their lives. Many of them have lost a lot until they achieved their goals, but they have always been ready to risk it all.

Things That Millionaires Won't Tell You but Will Agree Definitely On.

14. They hate wasting things

Whether its time, money or any other resource, millionaires will not waste a single chunk of anything. In one report, a successful founder of a company said:

> *"I still collect all the tiny pieces of soap and put them together into one bar. I still squeeze the toothpaste tube. And I grow my own vegetables".*
>
> – August Turak, net worth $24 million.

Conclusion

Monetalia *"The Guide to Achieve Financial Success"* can drastically change your financial situation. If you believe that you have a small budget, empty pockets or the life that you have not envisioned for yourself, this book will change your life. The advice in this book has been tried and proven by many individuals who have been highly satisfied.

Even in my own, personal experience, I can confirm that this book is highly effective. The advice in this book should be adopted by everyone seeking to change his boring life. If you are tired from *"working just to survive"* and you want to *"work to live a good life"* then this book will definitely give you the life you want.

Dear reader, thank you for choosing this book. Once you achieve the results this book is promising, do not thank me. You were the one who changed everything yourself, since your mind is capable of changing everything.

Things That Millionaires Won't Tell You but Will Agree Definitely On.

I want to thank my assistant writer named **Filip Dimkovski** who helped me a lot in the creation of this book.

Thank you dear reader, good luck to you!

Book Disclaimer

No part of this eBook may be reproduced or transmitted in any form or by any means, electronic or mechanical, including photocopying, recording or by any information storage and retrieval system, without written permission from the author.

The information contained within this eBook is strictly for educational purposes. If you wish to apply ideas contained in this eBook, you are taking full responsibility for your actions.

The author has made every effort to ensure the accuracy of the information within this book was correct at time of publication. The author does not assume and hereby disclaims any liability to any party for any loss, damage, or disruption caused by errors or omissions, whether such errors or omissions result from accident, negligence, or any other cause.

The methods describe within this eBook are the author's personal thoughts. They are not intended to be a definitive set of instructions for this project. You may discover that there are other methods and materials to accomplish the same end result.

www.ingramcontent.com/pod-product-compliance
Lightning Source LLC
Chambersburg PA
CBHW030517220526
45464CB00006B/2837